WIND *and* HILLS

WIND and HILLS

poems by
Marguerite Costigan

SHANTI ARTS PUBLISHING
BRUNSWICK, MAINE

Wind and Hills

Published by Shanti Arts Publishing

Designed by Shanti Arts Designs

Cover image: Pattanan (AI) / 739698818 / stock.adobe.com

Shanti Arts LLC
193 Hillside Road
Brunswick, Maine 04011
shantiarts.com

Printed in the United States of America

ISBN: 978-1-962082-35-8 (softcover)

Library of Congress Control Number: 2024943217

To Beverly Gingg, creator of the Learning Among the Oaks (LATO) nature program for elementary and middle school children

CONTENTS

III THE FIELD POEMS

IV THE RANCHOS

V POINTS WEST

VI A FEW SEASONS

VII TURNING FOR HOME

Acknowledgments

The author wishes to extend her thanks to the editors of the following publications in which these works previously appeared, some in altered form:

Solo Voyage (edited by Marsha de la O, David Oliveira, and Phil Taggart, and published by Glenna Luschei): "Autumn"

Corners of the Mouth: A Celebration of Thirty Years at the Annual San Luis Obispo Poetry Festival (edited by Kevin and Patti Sullivan, and published by Deer Tree Press): "Jenny's Canyon"; "The Nokomis Fritillary"; and " Resolve."

"The Field Poems" were printed as a limited run of ten broadsheets to be displayed as part of the author's multimedia exhibition *Portrait of an Open Field,* a merged artistic and scientific show, displayed in libraries, galleries, museums, and classrooms up and down the central California coast— Monterey to Ventura counties. *Portrait of an Open Field* was funded in part by an NEA (National Endowment for the Arts) grant through the SLO County Arts Council, and the author is very grateful for the local and national support of science and the arts—both!

I

OPENINGS

NIGHT WINDOW

Sat there like a fledgling
near-naked in bare quills
my heart's fist quaking me

Wide white windowsill
Double-hung panes gone liquid
from all that time leaking through

My irises gathering in
all of it, the out-there and
the within, the light

of a million suns just arriving,
galaxy a white arc spanning darkness
the flames, the glowing remnants

stinging my eyes wide open
centers spinning, wheeling, homing
on the marrow of my dreams:

the Pleiades, Cassiopeia
Pegasus and Orion
Cygnus, Sagittarius—

I plotted my future by them
flung out a seine of wishes
and drew in black-diamond waters

my heart is still drinking from
flung wings still hovering
soul finding its own face in

all that Being.

KOLOB CANYONS

—at Zion National Park, Utah

So much beauty
it takes hold of and shakes you
like a quaking aspen,
it sinks clawed fingers into your throat
so that you want to screeeeeam until
your rib-bones shatter, your breast cracks open,
it makes you want to laugh, sing, dance
crazy as a broken-limbed marionette
with its strings tied to *everything . . .*

fills you so you want to spill over, heave
to make more room, more *room* for it all,
so much *beauty!* It ruins you
like the Virgin face to face with the Dragon,
St. George gone to gobbets and splinters
all around you,
but the *Dragon!* its furnace of a mouth
opening into the hunger of your soul
to be filled, *filled!* by
such awesome, flaming, shimmering,
singing beauty, oh
so much, so much damn
Beauty!

RESOLVE

In this forever landscape
of redrock and cedar,
sky wide as heartbreak,
riverbottom willows
more golden than sun-ball,

I must be something different
than what I brought with me,
this inadequate vessel
cracked and time-checkered,
I must be made over:

I must be something bigger
to swallow such beauty—
buttes melting downslope
in pastels and pebbles,
rocks tall as battlements
riven by lightning,
ridge upon ridgeline
ranging the horizon—

I must be something braver
than eagles and ravens,
I must be something harder
than canyons and hogbacks,
I must be something sharper
than reefs running tilted
horizon to horizon . . .

I must be something stronger
than iron or whetstone,
I must be something wilder
than coyotes and pumas,

I must be something purer
than the fire every evening
that creeps up the red slopes,
flame against cobalt,
cerulean, viridian,
till night puts it out again ...

I must be something loyal
as the dawn that relights this
dawn after dawning,
the dark breathing out again
before breathing in.

CREATION

Oh may I be cleansed by all the winds of Earth,
may I be scrubbed of stubbornness,
be abraded of these scars by the rough tongues
of desert sandstorms,
be sculpted by mountain scree,
free of the hopeless yearning of river stones,
polished by tumbled boulders
till I've lost this chitin carapace,
shed this brittle coating
of face and form—to be shapeless, waiting
to be blown, flung, scattered, a worthless seed:

May I be naked and hairless as a newborn thing,
trusting my embryo heart to find its own rhythm,
among mountains as mothers,
oceans as soul-mates,
the endless changes of Nature as inevitable
as moods and fits and lovers: may I know Her
as fish, as bird, as stegosaur, as mammal,
even as myself; may I deeply understand
that She's not done with me, yet—
that I'm still in the making.

SUMMER CREEK

Oh there is nothing I would rather do
than exactly this: clean as a cut edge
it slices me apart, into tree-canopy,
into a thousand leaves, my heart aswim
in actinic sunlight, blackbirds shattering
the nerve-strung air, that near-impossible cobalt
stung with thrusting twigs, swelling my eyes
with colored clumps of song—oh there is nowhere
I would rather be right now than simply here
in this fat and open palm, this rich explosion
of four-in-the-afternoon, sitting at creekside
in this little City's heart, the air warm-cool,
the light hanging pendulous from my hands,
the traffic a soft song beneath the birds,
the water-murmur, the sounds from my own chest—
that deep susurrus, yes! oh yes, yes!
to the ongoing deeper rhythm of love! love!

II

IN THE OLD TONGUES

FROM THE ZEPHYR, FOLLOWING THE COLORADO

I.   Canyon

You must whisper
going through this narrow place:
The gods fling stones here
down grayrock walls
into a river green
with swallowed secrets.
They trade old trickster-stories,
laughing in sudden landslides—
hear those echoes?
The gods love bitter jokes.
Holes in the rock walls
yawn into nightmare faces;
cracks open everywhere;
the rocks melt and re-form,
slithering lower down
into red-ochre dust,
the dust the Old Ones painted
dead faces with.
You must go slyly, here:
The trickster gods change shape
so suddenly.
You must go softly, here:
They might spy you
perched like a dragonfly
on a river boulder,
flexing your filmy wings—
so little, so temporary.
Whisper your whole life over
to yourself,
to firm, to fix it:
When they laugh,
you might blow away.

II.   Plateau

Out of the birth canal
of the Great Divide,
running, like everything living,
to the Pacific,
we follow her, roadway-tied,
we follow her, S-curved, looping,
back-doubling, slender as dream is,
as willful purpose is,
feeling the pressure
of wind against glass, against
the stippled surface
of her own green-white, boulder-dappled
coldness,
sliding across the plateau
before Grand Junction.
Heavy we sit with words, with
carried metal,
awkward as children happening on
a goddess,
naked, at bathing: Stripped of our sexes
and weapons,
with nothing left to win,
we follow her dazedly, noses to windows,
tongues in our pockets, soundlessly
we follow her,
this river pressing her length against
the landscape,
this river braiding her fingers among
the cottonwoods,
this river, scattering light
like a sequinned lady.

III. Mesa

You can tell
the Old Ones lived here.
Broad green, in a sheath of leaves
the river stretches,
ripe woman with swollen belly,
lined with the lips of strata,
pink, peeled back
into small mouths always parting,
always beckoning
downstream, downhill, down-time
beyond this moment
that we move suspended in,
green tourists, passing,
eyes glued to the mesas,
where the wind
fingers the dust of the Old Ones,
the Anasazi,
who knew this river when
she had a name
no one remembers now.
Hard on the skyline
the broken mesas tower,
their pink and orange fingers
pointing up-time, down-time,
but always pointing
into the wind.
Fingers glued to our tickets
we sit, we watch them passing:
room after room of shadows
in the cave-mouths,
eyeless windows,
doorless arches,
empty stairways
of the painted-mesa country.

Hands gripping our purses
we sit and watch them passing—
who must have been like us:
who built these cities,
who lived, like us, in cities
the sun still sets on.

IV. Desert

Between these buttes
old crone river runs brown,
muttering her Spanish name,
Colo-rado, the Red One.
Lines of rock crawl beside her,
flattening
into faded ribbons, pink, orange,
beige, dun, gray—
a buried seabed lifted into the sky,
spread-eagle to the sky,
with all her secrets showing.
This waste is somehow fitting
for us, who have dammed and sold
her liquid reaches,
as if she were a slave.
We ride now, paper masters,
we who have drunk and eaten
everything,
we who think
there is no shame in barrenness,
if it serves people . . .
We sit here empty,
feeling the sudden loss, the caves
inside us,
feeling the wind grieving
in the rails.

Out of the desert mirror of
our own making,
the ghost of Old Woman Sea,
the First Mother,
looks emptily back at us.
It all fits.
It's like the water withdrew
ages ago, fleeing
into the west,
and we are all—rocks, river,
and the railroad—
helplessly
hurrying after it.

AT LIMEKILN CREEK

I.   The Camp

We all come here
bearing original magic.
Us: the fire,
the wheel, the metal rod,
the spoken word.
But the Others came before us.
In the night
when the Black-and-Silver Masked Ones
come slipping down to wash
their small, dark, patient fingers
in the Creek,
I swear I can almost hear them
muttering incantations
between their teeth.

II.   The Creek

In this darkness
loud with the voice of the Creek
of the Two Mothers,
I lie with the Mothers
at my head and feet:
the Great Mother Sea
and the Mother that is the Mountain
of the Sur Coast,
feeling them joined and singing
through my throat,
one at my head, the other at my feet,
and my body the Creek between them,
birthed, engorged,
the Creek of the Fallen Redwoods
and the White Limestone:

O this is harder than stone
than hearts can harden to
than breasts can turn themselves into

    O this is deeper, this long
    and rhythmic singing

O this is higher and more still
than the first light touching

    O this is lower than everything
    this dark is salt-laced

O this sings true

    O this rings truly

O Air-sweet

    O Water-bitter

O Dipper-song

    O Star-spill

O Sea-swimmer

    O Stone-grinder

Greet you

    I greet you

All night long back and forth they sing
through the loud voice of the Creek
this love, this acknowledging,
each to the other.

III. The Falls

What mountain and ocean cannot do,
the sky does:
light touching rock, and turning it
into fire.
Dawn on the Big Sur Mountain
teaches you things
you thought you had forgotten.
The voice of the Shaman
of the Clay-stone Falls
echoes inside you:
this is his mark you feel
upon your forehead,
upon your chin.
You swallow this dream like
a bright song,
and take it away with you.

SNOWY OWL

This is winter:
the limbs like trees
in an old orchard;
the smell of rotting apples
like wine in the nostrils,
like old, spilled blood.

There is no food for the tongue
in this bitter place,
a station for the mind only,
where the senses sleep
like willows under snow,
under the thick cover
of ritual forgetting.

Only the wind sings here
its thin, far song of regret.
Only the pale light here
of ice, of the moon on wings
of snow-white owls.
Only the death of questions.

Look to the few drift-fences
bounding the edge of vision,
how the snowfields swallow them
in a flat returning,
closing in again and again.

This is where reasons stop.
This is where all the fires
are meaningless.
This: ground-zero.

Look for the white owl-feathers
in the thickets of snow.
Look for the soundless wings
brushing a fall of powder
from dead tree-limbs.

Go make your cold way slowly,
body in hand,
dragged like a dogsled harness,
all feeling gone.

The mind is a terrible thing:
you grin; you bear it.

Creep gently over this snow.
You will feel the white owl following
in your footsteps.
You will turn and meet his eyes:
so black,
so gold.

SONG OF ICE-BRINGER, GRANDMOTHER OF THE NORTH WIND

It is necessary, this resting.
Under the ice the locked field
grows still, has itself to itself,
does the long, slow work of remembering.
Under the frozen soil the deep water
goes hollow, sings to itself
of the long night, a dark throat humming
its own ending.
It is necessary.
What beauty it is cannot be told.
What rest it is can be felt only
as the heart feels itself.
Find in memory the old key to unlock it.

Such is the mind's winter:
the packing and unpacking of boxes
in a crowded attic,
the self gone far upstairs
to be alone with its thinking.
Rest in this, rest.
The winter ice is patient,
blue and white, the slow fire
of diamonds, of centuries.
Rest, rest.
The resting is the best gift
it has to give you.

Marsh Hawk in the Valley of the Hot Springs

Listen:
running water.
The day breaks
the hawk's falling
on the frosted grass,
iced with a caking
of ground-crust,
thin and slippery
with intention.
The smell of the winegold colors
inside your brain
is an old tasting,
a long and forgotten one.
Sit by the brookside
dreaming the hawk's falling,
the tilt, the recovery,
the caked grasses
frosted with sulfur-oxides,
running golden
with rimed light.
What the hawk takes
is meaningless.
It will become hawk,
it will become grasses,
it will become all of us:
In the ending of itself
is this pitiless
becoming...
But there is no ending to it:
it just changes, then continues
to go on.

FROM THE SHE-CROW: WHAT SHE KNOWS OF THE USES OF GRAVITY

Living among those
who believe only in clouds
makes my wings ache,
makes my feet curl
into tree-limbs.

The air is full of them,
mouths thick with words,
eyes hard with measurement:
how high, how fast, how best
to keep from falling.

The sky is full of them:
wind-spirits, speed-spirits,
breaking out of solid form,
mating in mid-motion,
quick and flailing.

My feet were made for ground.
I walk like a furred animal,
planting my soles gravely,
rocking from side to side
my black body.

I fly when necessary,
beating against the wind,
crying my discontent among
the falcons, the hummingbirds,
the orioles.

I fly because I have to:
to drop from a wise height
these kernels I crack open.
I know all there is to know
about falling.

From the She-Crow: What She Knows of Love as Trickster

Fence your heart
with cactus, with poison ivy,
with creosote four-by-fours:
the coyote will muscle in,
digging with snout and paws,
ragged brush waving.

Hire a lineman
to ride the stubborn fenceline,
armed with barbwire, shovel,
and varmint rifle. Tell him
to backfill burrows, to harden
the air with bullets.

Tell him to shoot
to kill, then hang the carcass,
gutted and rotting, spread-eagle
on the fence. Tell him to do this
as many times, as many shots
as he has to.

You will soon be
surrounded by carcasses.
They will keep coming, one coyote
after another. You will see them
beyond the fenceline, running,
alive and laughing.

You will see them
fall to the spade,
the bullet, fall to the wire
that hangs them. You will hear
them baying at noon and midnight,
praying, singing.

You will live
battered by carcasses
of your own invention. You will give
no quarter. You will be firm.
You will never be
taken in.

Till the night
the lineman finally finds you,
ass in the air, eyes set
on the black horizon,
nose pressed
hard to your own fenceline,
digging, digging.

FROM THE SHE-CROW: WHAT SHE STOLE FROM THE UNIVERSE

Loosen my tongue
with the flint knife of your thinking.
Loosen my wings
with the wind of your contempt.
Loosen my entrails
with loneliness.

I will rise to this illusion.
I will fly
in widening circles, high
above this canyon,
my eyes as hard and open
as the stars.

There will be no lightning.
There will be dead rivers
beneath my feet,
scars and red bruises on
spread-eagle landscape.
There will be grieving.

You can believe
whatever death you want to.
You can burn out
the white stars one by one,
swallowing light
in nova and black hole.

I have spent years
learning to see in darkness,
singing myself to sleep
with this split tongue,
waiting in dead air
for the winds of home.

I will not drop
this kernel that I carry.
I will not stop
the heartbeat of these wings.
I will not let
this love you gave me, go.

*TUQUSKI WA SUWA:** Bear and Child

—for the sculptor Paula Zima

This place still remembers the Other People.
It isn't taken in
by crosses, Japanese carp, Spanish roof-tiles,
roses that have forgotten
their Chinese childhoods
under American names.

It has waited patiently
under the English grass, the concrete pathways,
the space-age contrails
marking commuters halfway to LA,
under the steady dinning of the traffic.

It still remembers the Old Ones,
silver-shouldered,
that ran like flowing mountains,
and the Younger Ones
that shelled and pounded acorns
and laughed . . .
This place, it remembers Them laughing.

Yesterday the shape of a Bear
and the shape of a She-Child
of the Chumash People,
welded in bronze, set among native stones
in the Mission Plaza fountain—
we brought Them back to stay.

*From the native Chumash for "Bear and Child"

And today the long drought breaks!
Their shapes are washed by rain, rain! Again
it pours itself whispering
over the humped shoulders, the bronze skin,
whispering all it remembers
in celebration, whispering
the native names, the almost-forgotten names
of the Other People.

Changing the Names

The valley called Zion
that canyon of the Virgin River,
lost its name Makuntaweap
when the white-skins took over

who drew crosses everywhere
with their deliberate fingers:
on orange walls, rust-stained,
in hidden caves; wrote language

strangely, not like pictographs
walking into distance—
Lizard, Crow, Blanket-Folk
eroding into silence

None speak now of acorns
reed-grass, fingered clay
dug-up roots, deerskins
painted, wrapped to lay in

Nights beside the fire-holes
snow upon the shoulders
of frozen gods, the waters
wild beyond the shelters

The river curving, carving in
then in sunlight shrinking
on summer days, burrowing
its own bed, digging in

Bank-beavers scurrying
sacred blossom blooming
cactus fruit reddening
foretold days coming

when Paiute and blue-clad ones
each other's blood angered
gentle horses, fierce men
long days of red danger

Fences and cattle-runs
longhorns and metal knives
fleeing the ancient lands
following the River's curves

carrying, inside, the Tongues
the story-songs, the buryings
the Timeless Names—not quite
but oh, almost—forgetting.

From the Warner Valley

—at Lassen Volcanic National Park, California

Listen, an entire valley full of whispers:
tree-whisper, water-whisper, low-grass whisper.
Listen and I can finally hear it, here:
the original voice, the First of Singers singing
in this wind-kissed valley.

Something here thought the original thought
of speech, of singing, long before tongues or throats,
long before ears attentive, swiveling,
a fine-sprung forest of hairs telling
the wind's direction.

Long before all this was, this whispering was,
through the pine boughs, singing down-mountainside,
sunset and sunrise, singing into the valley-bottom
the low-blown song of movement, the song of being
one place and then another place, and touching

sides of boulders in passing, brows of stones
on hillsides, jaw-ridges of outcroppings,
singing this touch, this movement, and its passing,
sliding down-mountain to the valley floor
to gather into a pool, a pond of singing,

thick with the possibilities of tongues and ears:
a pool of song that births its own listening.
Oh I sing it back, the song I have taken in!
Listen: the pencil whispers against this paper,
the wind sings in my ear-hairs, in the whorls

of my inner ears, the pines the grass the waters
sing: Listen! this is what ears are for,
what Song is for! This,
the First Singer, singing!
Oh I sing it back, the Song I was shaped to hear.

III

THE FIELD POEMS

FIELD SPIRIT 1: THE FIELD IN RAIN

Oh today, this soft rain
under opossum-colored clouds
calls me forth, dripping
time like old moss, these dry limbs
(straw, silvered by all the lying still)
feeling the wind now from the wet ocean,
the storm-track trooping
these silver needles in
to prick me awake again—a ghost in weeds;
a skin of all the grasses that ever grew here;
a skeleton of stones;
fingers of lupine-fruits
bursting into black pebbles
that roll forever downhill;
a skull of serpentine, the veins of this mountain
my deathbed lies on—my bed that is this field:
I rise, the Spirit of This Field,
holding open my lost, my impossible
eyeholes,
summoned by the first, the forgiving
winter rain.

FIELD SPIRIT 2: THE FIELD IN BLOOM

Whatever I am at other times, now
I am female,
I am all green but the blossoms
starring my hair:
yellow and lavender clusters,
tiny red and white winkings,
long wavy-edged ribbons of soap-plant leaves
weaving the stems together,
and the goldenstars, ah!
my converging everywhere eyes,
and my concha belt of the orange-gold coins
of poppies . . .
Whatever I was before is meaningless.
I am full of grain, I am full of ripening lupines,
I am full of the sweet sap
of a million grasses,
I am spilling wind-in-grass music.
I dance a forever-dance, my flowered limbs
swaying and bending, heavy with animals,
with eggs of birds, with human fingerprints.
I am the flesh of dreams!
All at once, now and everyplace,
I swell, I ripen.

FIELD SPIRIT 3: THE CUT FIELD

Thought to beat me, didn't you?
But I am a spiny Trickster
hiding these other costumes up my sleeve.
Cut off my beard—I turn Buckeye;
bury my music—I'm Crow,
flapping the heat-wave air
back into your face,
laughing my August laugh
at your pettiness.
Purple spineflower blooms best
in open sunlight:
the metal-green, frenzied bees
have you to thank
who took the knife to my skin
in fire-fear . . .
Cicadas buzz
on my drowsy summer breast;
my pockets overflow wasps
and butterflies . . .
Do you feel this laugh?
Do you see who laughs the best?

Field Spirit 4: The Field in Moonlight

Oh silver and lavender
as dreams, as wishes,
I open my eyes under a full moon
that rises slow and round over the shoulders
of the sleeping Santa Lucias.
Pine-needles whisper, eucalyptus leaves
mutter their night-songs...
Now I am the Hunter,
the Watcher, the Silver-Haired
who glides with the Owl on-shoulder,
its dark-moon eyes
staring, its eared head swiveling, swiveling.
I am the One who prowls the meadow-edges;
I am the One who sees in all directions.
I am the Limpid-Eyed, the Cloven-Hoofed,
the Bandit-Masked, the utterly Silent-Feathered.
I am the One who questions, Who? Who?
under your very window.
I am the One who points the silent finger
that troubles you in your dreams.
I am the One who drops the single feather
you stumble on, sleep-walking, in the dawn.

What the Field Sings to the Sky
Before the Bulldozers

You are not now the things you were—
          on change all living hangs:
I have been other things before,
          will be still other things . . .

I have been ocean-bed and rock,
          have risen and been buried,
have stood as mountain, crumbled back
          to pebbles, river-carried.

This isn't yet the end of it,
          this being scraped and covered,
sold for whatever price they get
          to keep me building-tethered.

Oh but the covering is hard:
          the Sky no longer Lover,
the centuries of nail and board
          imprisoned from the weather . . .

If I must soon be bodiless,
          will you forget the passion?
If I must grow another face,
          will you remember this one?

IV

THE RANCHOS

AT SUR SUR RANCH

I climb the oak-furred hillside toward the sky,
into the slurred scream of the hawk hunting.
Downslope the fog dissolving layers of cypress flags.
Gray boulders gilded with fallen laurel leaves
in a hill-notch. Ghost of water. Promises
of streams. I breathe out, and the fog tatters.
I breathe in. Bay-laurels exhale.
Sulphur butterfly sipping a patch of mud,
pattern-winged flies flanking him.
Footprints: bobcat, raccoon, fox, towhee, quail,
deer, men, in the road's beige talcum.
Dust the unnameable color of buckwheat blossoms.
Thick stillness. Hundred-degree air. Spots of shade,
like the sky's underbelly, sun-shot full of holes.
Upslope the high tops baking in the afternoon.
Fog like a pearl afghan waiting downslope.
Between, dirt-colored deer lie hidden, dreaming,
chewing the morning's cud. Evening waiting.
When I leave, I have to wake something inside me
that fell asleep in the deep bay-laurel shade:
something that has no words, just ears and eyes.
I sling myself over my shoulder, a drowsy lizard,
my boot-heels slipping and digging all the way down.
Pygmy oaks, speechless, sift the dust of my trail
in an ancient rite of thinking and rethinking.
Bay-laurel leaves in my pocket scent my brain.
Downslope, motorcycles racket off up the Coast Road.

Autumn at the Baldwin Ranch

—for Mary Alice

Shh, be still, listen: the red-tail screaming.
It is mid-November, a year of little acorns;
the rains have not yet come. You are in the meadow,
the Horse Meadow, beyond the bluestone fenceline.
It is early morning, gray-violet in the shadows
that lie across the field. The field is flaxen,
the bleached-straw of a child's hair, or a ghost's;
dried horse-dung in it, the quaking-grass atremble,
the jays scratching in the shadows. It is early,
but the late smell in the air, that thread of crickets,
troubles your chest. Bright light sings from the maples,
the sycamores; the sky-light flashes metallic
off the bay-laurel leaves. Quail in the oak woods
chuckle and bubble; a file of wild turkeys,
shimmering bronze-on-steel-blue, tiptoes past.

Listen: the high, clear screaming of the red-tail
circling the bowl of the valley, above the gray pines,
above the red peaks, above the hidden source
of the San Carpojo Creek, above the bluestone,
circling: the valley below like a stone mortar
with the pestle of creek. He sees with his hawk's eyes;
you see with the eyes of your heart. A quick shiver
rattles your sleeves: a sudden stamp at the wood-edge—
a woman? a ghost? You stare at the deep shadow,
willing it open, that gate between thing and thing:
and the place's spirit enters you. Ripe as the grasses,
pungent as laurel, round as an acorn, it opens:
this love. This LOVE. And you kneel in the Horse Meadow,
under the scream of the red-tail, weeping, grateful
to leave a piece of your heart here, in the quaking-grass.

AT THE AVENALES RANCH

—for Jane McClellan

I feel you watching from the curtained window.
You were past 90 and you lived here yet,
hours from town, along old Pozo Road,
then up the river-bed below the Machesnas
into this wandering canyon, where I sit
today, painting. It was your final spring,
and you knew it, April sunlight glittering
on the willows by the creek. Was it as cold,
I wonder, as today? Spreading my paints,
I shiver, rub my hands, pull up my collar—
I still can feel your stare. The sunlight flashes
white as a blizzard on the sycamore
at the bottom of the yard. I feel you smile,
remembering, comparing that old giant
once, to yourself: it flashes lightning-white,
columnar, from the road; but from the creek-bed
you can see it's hollow, clear up to the sky—
black, fire-cored—the opposite of you,
you thought, whose failing, aging shell surrounded
a core solid and stubborn. Listening,
both me and you: the crickets on that hill
forever chanting evening, even at noon;
the horses whickering; the black-tailed deer
stamping below the oaks; the falling-water
song of a canyon wren that lights atop
the ridgepole of the barn, faces due east,
then opposite, hurling its tumbling whistle
in both directions. Hearing him, I think:
you heard him, that last spring—I think it grew
inside you, the certain knowledge of the end
caught in that falling song; I think you knew.

The curtain flutters. I hear you suddenly
inside my temples: *"Look! The way I looked!*
Look back upon your life and be ecstatic!
I loved my life here, and I know you feel it!"
My breath trembles; the brush leaps in my fingers,
tracing the willow-limbs that you saw greening.
I feel your triumph running like the grasses,
singing like crickets, *"Joy!"* After a lifetime
solid as wood, *joy!* to be going down,
to be cored out, like the sycamore, at last,
your heart falling, falling, like the canyon wren.

Late Afternoon at Santa Margarita Ranch

Sit you down in the shade of the blue oaks,
their long-legged shadows racing away
from the westering sun, toward evening.
Feel the earth beneath you as if being held
in a mother's careful hand.
The land, your body,
still as the setting sun.

Now close your eyes,
the one sense that distracts you.
Sweep away thoughts, dust
that scatters to air,
only dust. Feel your breath
filling your chest, your belly,
long out and in. Out and in.
Feel the earth keeping you still, feel the gravity
holding everything down. Feel the wind
brushing against your cheeks.
Spread out your closed-eye senses:

Nearby, grasshoppers chirring, the afternoon trills
of crickets merging to dusk-song,
the rustle of wind fingering dry grasses,
a separate rustle—closed-eyed, you know
it's an animal,
the sounds faint but steadier than the wind—
what is it? A gopher snake? A gray fox
sliding past, his eyes keenly watching you,
his whiskers all aquiver? You notice
the sound fades. And now you hear the birds:

The raspy caw of a crow stationed overhead
as lookout; happy chatter of red finches
and the plaintive murmur of mourning doves
saying *coo AAH, coo coo coo*—
refugees hiding here
from the southern ring-necks, who've overtaken
their native haunts;
the rust-sided chickadees repeating, repeating
their own names;
and high up, high, the *kir kir*
of a red-shouldered hawk, circling.

The wind is cooler now—you feel it drying
the sweat left on your neck from the afternoon.
You stretch out your hand, blind, and feel, feel
the pebbles jostle beneath your palm;
dry leaves crisped and leathered
from the blue oaks; the feathery fronds of wild fennel;
the prickle of thistle; the delicate stems of wild-aster
bending beneath your fingers.

The fennel-scent comes across a second after
your bruising touch—
it comes to you pungent and acrid.
You pluck a frond and taste it, mint and acid,
deep notes like thunder warm your tongue and throat,
nibbling softly at the edges.
And the fragrance steals your nostrils utterly.
All you feel is these three senses
bundled into one.
Breathe out, in; out and in.

The dusk is coming. You can feel it in
the wind, in the whistling wings
of mourning doves. Back of your shoulders
the brazen sun is setting.
You open your eyes to olive green, gray-blue,
red-gold, all shimmering around you,
clean of detail—all pure color
that kisses and lifts your eyelids. You feel
what can only be named
as ecstasy.

It is still, as the dusk comes slipping
over the dry grass. You can feel
horizon to horizon,
how the ochre fields stretch away from you.
You, a two-legged satellite
walking across the earth
with what can only be named
as love.

AT THE DALIDIO RANCH, BEFORE THE SUBDIVISION

The soft twitter of swallows in the air
over this fallow field that stretches low
and long to the hills on the horizon:

swallows weaving and dancing, arcing through
and past each other's trails like acrobats,
falling all for the hell of it, on wings.

Small yellow sulphur butterflies, cabbage whites,
and dusky skippers among the flowering weeds—
telegraph weed, chicory, prickly sow-thistle—

at least this soil still grows something, at least
flies and grasshoppers still rise to the swallows' fall
to be taken on the wing. At least the windbreak

of blue gums stands, shading a wooden shed
that slowly fades to the colors of dirt, dead leaves,
swallow feathers and the dust of butterflies.

I close my eyes to slow this surfeit of thought;
imagine myself sinking, a larval cicada,
deep into warm soil, between roots and stones—

a 17-year cicada, sleeping beneath
the cries of swallows, the blood of trees on the wind,
the soil soon to be paved, tamped and hardened;

I imagine myself sleeping far past the years
of emergence, my red eyes closed, keeping the dreams
of swallows and sky, of weeds and butterflies—

Somebody has to keep this, why not me?—
when swallows fight for eave-space for their young;
when weeds are cracking sidewalks; when butterflies

are photographs in books mothers read to children
who cannot believe such things ever flew, who help
their fathers knock down swallow mud-nests, so
the house-paint's safe, the resale value's unbroken.

Painting *August Afternoon, Blue Oak Grove*

—for Colleen and Raymond Mattison

There's a trail through the oaks of East Santa Margarita
Ranch-land, made for the children of local ranchers
and merchants to learn of their native environment,
its history, wild and tamed; its secret shades . . . .

It winds and loops, barely seen at times, through forage
and poison oak, past deer-trail and badger-hollow,
past blue oaks, rounded and full, trailing their branches
low to the earth—unlike their valley cousins

that scribble limbs high against the sky and trail
long tresses, like extra fingers. The blues are women
in full-blown skirts, hiding the earth in their shade.
We wander up there, one August day, a painter

and an "artist's *sherpa*," carrying packs and canvases
and what we assume is "plenty of ice-cold water
to last one afternoon!" North SLO County
in August—the native ghosts must have giggled at us

as we set up easels, pulled on our wide-brimmed sunhats.
I spread out my landscape-pigments, Cezanné-grayed
for distance, squinted my eyes into summer heat
rising from oven-baked grass—and set to work.

No wind, no sound, no red-tail hawk or vulture
punctured the pitiless, maddening glare of sky.
No breath but dust on the leaves, no rasp of locusts.
Only the scratch of my brush against our eardrums.

I tried to be true to my training by starting two
realistic echoes, in just that many dimensions:
blue sky (like verdigrised copper), blue under-tree shadows
(like gas-stove flames!), blue shadows among blue oaks,

blue sky-holes burning through them—but it was wrong,
all *wrong!* The long hours ticked away, getting hotter:
one hundred and ten degrees in North County shade
and my paper blasting white into my charred gaze—

the water long gone, my jaw set grim and firm;
my eyes thin slits letting only the shapes of things
into my brain—and suddenly I gave in,
threw away the training, " ... paint what you *see* ... " I tore

fresh paper out of its pad; I splashed its whiteness
with the blazing heat of the sun, my own sweat urging
my fingers to "paint what you *feel!*" I splattered shade
with flaming violet, lit a brush-fire of orange

and red in the simmering grass; I burned heat-shimmer
of sodium-flare yellow sky-holes into the olive-
and-sage of the blue oak mounds, setting them dancing;
I picked up wads of yellow and *painted sky*

like it felt! my throat, my lips, my eyes, my tongue
gone dry as the lack of wind. I shimmered and burned
like a torch, lighting my paper with the landscape
as if with a soundless fire—and it felt *good!*

So good, not to be bowing and compromising;
not to be gentle, but to be *true to life*
when life is ablaze with heat, when colors turn
upside-down, on their heads, as clear as children,

as vivid, as scorching, as hot as the metal sun!
And a cool breeze licked at my hands as I sweated the finish:
the fine, pale ghosts of the wild oats starting to lean
and tremble and dance, in the welcome air of dusk.

AT THE CHIMINEAS RANCH

—for Mike Post

Sunset, and we gravitate toward the cookhouse,
pulled by invisible strings—smoked bricks, camaraderie
after the long day of struggle and solitude.
Late sun lies orange on pale adobe walls,
on the inset tiles outlining the garden surround.
It is spring, with flaming orioles in the trees
that carry heavy tresses of bloom, like long hair
falling in white and purple masses about them,
trembling, shedding petals on the wind.
On the overlooking hill, the cairn fires back
the sun's last rays, then fades into indigo
beneath its guardian oaks—the Boy lies there,
the one who wanted always to stay with the land:
His wish was granted. A quarter-moon is rising
high to the east, unnoticed; the horses stand
gazing like bronzes; the roaming cattle settle
to grind their cud, dark eyes fixed on the horizon.

How many fires were stoked at the Chimineas
we have no way of counting—how many hours
marked only by ache and strain, rut and routine,
and the lift of rest at the end, the cattle-gates shut,
the stock corralled, the slopes left to the elk
and the loose elk-fences; the hay-bales piled against
the coming drought, the wildflower-petals closing,
the dogs or foxes barking in the distance—
immeasurable silence settling in around
the fences, buildings, pickups, animals
and humans all alike. Wind from the Boneyard
of broken metal, a history of machines
all vulnerable, in the end—a wind comes stealing
over the oak-studded hilltops, pools around

the adobe arches, tiptoes through the shadows
humming faint twilight songs, while overhead
the galaxy splashes pale across the Universe.

It slowly wheels us in—warm fire, drink
and solid food; laughter and weariness
envelop us like ghostly hands on shoulders,
caressing, soothing... How do you tell in words
the spell of a place? how you fall in love with land
as if it were the known body of a lover,
commensurate with your own? There are no words
but the singing in the fire-grate, or the yipping
of coyotes in the darkness, far outside
this circle of human light... We fall asleep
flowing across the silvered slopes like running elk—
the slopes are quilts; the elk are hunted dreams.

V

POINTS WEST

BARBWIRE

Ran through my head all morning, the hard rise
and fall. Remembering prairie, Oklahoma,
dust to the horizon. On the fenceline
the split, spread-eagle carcass of a coyote.
That savagery. That emptiness. That pain.

Tornados far off, tunneling the sky:
the irrational made flesh, or at least form,
born out of thunderstorm. The long wait
for nothing. For everything. Red-orange grass
the only tongues for miles, whispering.

Running the strange shapes over in my hands:
spearhead, rowel, thorn, spur, bifurcate
with bitter rust. The red grass rustling
so slight it barely moves. The deep hoof-prints
of buffalo filled with dust. Barbwire, thin

as a line of blood. I grasp it with both hands,
spread it enough to slither through. I look back
over my shoulder: there, my red-lit skin
is hanging, impaled. What's left of me goes on,
spur, rowel, thorn. Bleeding, to the horizon.

Coyote Smelling Rain

Dry as the sky just now
high over Texas
in the drought of '06
eating dust and crow

Biting embedded slivers
out of my forepaws
like they burn the needles off
the prickly pear

Hugging the naked fenceline
I run dreaming
a scruff of fur and urine
a stubborn changeling

sniffing above the dust-devils
across the wasteland
the god's tears gathering
into sweet meaning

BURNING CEDARS IN THE HILL COUNTRY

Opened the front screen door to let in evening
and the smell of burning cedars filled the air,
resinous and regretful, red smoke-chimneys
leaning up-sky like skinny cumulus,
backlit by setting-sun light. Burning cedars
to clear the land for later filling in
with houses, backyards, pools, pets, dogs and horses
and goats and sheep and chickens. And always *people*,
always the buyers climbing over the ridges,
the agents, the acreage-signs, the developers,
the contractors, wirers, diggers, the concrete-mixers,
always the fuss and frenzy. A Texas cardinal,
his pale breast stained with spreading crimson, calls
from the cedar in my yard, gone dark against
the westering sun. My eyes are watering.
My throat is raw with grieving. On the wind
the blood of all those cedars ... Really, junipers:
they could make gin. They could make pickled berries
to marinate tough beef in. They could shade
the deer, the speckled longhorns. My nostrils tremble,
sucking that sharp, delirious odor in.
Behind my house, trees shudder in the wind
that comes up every evening, skittering stones
across the porch. I cough and sniffle, feeling
dead cedars swaying, lost landscape giving in.
Will they rake up those ashes in the morning,
I wonder now, or will they let them lie,
for wind and rain to scatter them? I fenced
my cedars in; nailed signs up: *No Trespassing*.
But the people come and come, they come, and come ....
It's times like this, I wonder why I'm trying.

FIRE-SEED, IN THE SIERRA

Dawn-fire glows
an ember wrapped in cobweb
and bedstraw
black-mold darkness
smoke-thick and smothering
everything

Fragile as light-wave
glimmer as
eyelid opening
tenuous and pale
anemic as faintness and
sleeper rising to
crack-cold and gray-dark
waking

Ember burgeoning
feeding memory
wanting
knowing
recognition

Dawn-fire
in this cold wilderness
fires everything

The Nokomis Fritillary

If voice had wings, I think they would be these:
pale tapestries of smoke and ashes, rising
from Temple ruins left by the Saracens
and Christians both, after the spasms of war

or love. They would be these, flitting translucent
over dead mountain grasses and tough hillocks
of lichened stone, over the varied olives
and grays of frost-line trees with stunted limbs.

That *this* has wings, smoke-blue and charcoal-stained
on a pale background, leached of vivid color
as if by tears for the long fall of moments
stubbornly flowing out of reach—I think

the remnants of such leaching would be these
time-tattered patterns, following some path
unknown to mind-front, tracing the soul's shape
against the air, transient as any leaf.

If this thin page could leave a single print
on air, like that high-mountain butterfly,
I would not mourn one ember of this poem,
knowing its ash, like that, would wing away.

In Arizona, Waiting

—for Rosanne and Jon Seitz

Rode us a drone of metal across the flatlands,
pressing our hands together, skin too warm
in the desert sun, the air too dry to cool us.
Blooded ocotillo whips, chollas unbroken

by boots or chaps, by hooves or human footsteps.
Saguaros raising desperate arms, white blossoms
like offered flesh to the unbroken blue
that arches us, unfeeling and unheeding.

We lick the sweat that runnels down our faces.
The rusted waste of distance: sienna, ocher,
lavender, old-gold, all rubbed together
on the light-recording canvas in our eyes.

Vultures circle a noon-hot sky, relentless
as ticking minutes. Within each other's grasp
we feel our heartbeats. Pressed against the glass
of taut-stretched skin, we feel the slow, deep cooling

of the interior fires that maintain us.
How do we breathe against the heat of deserts?
How shall we separate, and walk apart?
How do we keep the memory of water?

How will we be each other's golden seed
to sprout as promised after the thunderstorm,
after the salt of tears has buried us,
the flash-floods torn us loose, sowing the wind

with the infinite speckles of our memories?
We sit and gaze: the ruins of Casa Grande,
the tiny colored trains toiling the landscape,
the carefully pent-up reservoirs, the language

etched on the rocks, star-cacti caught in sand,
wild sheep with their slit-horizontal eyes,
coiled as sculptures, fired in bronze and dust.
Later, the end of water, of words, the sensing

of the cease of breathing ... Then, Afterward begins—
long days of nothing, nothing, and more nothing
as it all burns to ash, to emptiness.
The clocks tick madly on. The faded curtains

stir in an afterthought of air, the windows
blank eyeholes staring outward, closing inward.
Long drawn-out after-images: red of sandstone,
dried blood of ancient rivers, rocks of iron

on all the paths we walk, now. Metallic boulders
slickened with desert-varnish—all footing fails ...
Some timeless Later, slitted reptilian eyelids,
stiff with reluctance, crack all senses open:

whisper of dust across the open doorsills;
sob and flutter of doves in drooping palm-fronds;
dawn-gold light on the Superstition Mountains ...
faint in the distance the whispering of rain.

Monterey Pine Forest

—San Simeon State Park, California

The wind moving through these branches
spins a language
particular to no other place. The pines
scent the air with regret. The sound of whispers
rustles along the forest floor, faintly warning
of passing time. We step in separate trances,

our eyes shafted by light, by shifting shadow,
by the blank blue of the air between the trees
and the glimpses of far-off country, dim as dreams
suspended between dark trunks of thrust and piercing,
alive with slivered light flashing its needles
straight into consciousness.

Thud of our footfalls,
rush of breath in this whisper-spattered stillness.
Prickle-slung branches whip into our faces—
blackberry, wild rose. The scent of dying
along the wind; the banked wings of a buzzard
soundless above our heads. When we emerge

the hills look loving, the grass in tongue-lick patterns
lying flat against the full breasts of the slopes.
We stand like sunset horses, head to tail,
hearing the shape of the valley in our ears
yawning out wide and open.
We who could run forever stand as still

as the trees, catching the last light
in our fingers,
fine as the silk of thistles in the wind.
We are filled with love, of a wordless
and silent kind.

DUNE WALK

—*by Black Lake, Nipomo, California*

The dunes lie blooming under the pearl and gray
of a June sea-fog that kisses my bare face.
My fingers are hungry legs: I trail them lightly
across the bee-hung flowers of silver lupine,
small hairy, curling leaves feeling as fuzzy
as bees do—but the bees are busy and warm,
and the lupine still and cool. I touch beach-primrose,
each small and red-blotched petal; the Hooker's primrose
that straggles leggy and high at the outer margins
of this looping path—its petals are large, full-blown
as yellow sails.
                    There is no wind to carry
the full scents off—the sweetness pools around me
in the pearly summer air, filling my nostrils,
burrowing into my brain with wild-bee honey,
Monarda mint, dried seaweed, wild anise,
cakilé-mustard, and the faint tang of sweat
from my swinging arms . . .
                         I have always found
and loved wild places—but this one especially:
this place caught between sea and fields, between drought
and irrigation, between the feet of men
and of snowy plovers—this hummocky, silky-velvet
place, safe from the nearby waste of tarmac . . .
I sniff the air, wishing I were a mermaid.

HALEIWA

—North Shore, Oahu, Hawaii

Never did anything at all to deserve it. Came
as a magic surprise package, ribbons trailing:
palm fronds, bead-strung lehua-tree seeds,
reef out on the sun-cloud horizon,
cane and pineapple fields,
hidden waterfalls,
frozen lava turned underfoot
into slicing stone.

Lived there a year when I was just twenty.
It wrapped itself around me, a strange lover
I hardly dared to believe in.
Took me all that year
to see the differences between
the palm trees, to learn their common names:
coconut, date, palmetto, Asian,
queen and king. And the beautiful, alien flowers
woven into leis: *aloha,*
goodbye. And welcome.

When it's winter there,
when the sugarcane trucks run by
on the mountain roads,
and you see some ghost in the red-rust rain
bleeding down your fogged-in windows—
that is me, looking for Pelee's hair
on the Pali crest.

When you wake at night in a moonless dark
to feel
that pounding deep in your chest,
that thrumming echo
from the winter sea beating

against the reef, and you're questioning
the dark inside you—that sound is me.

When you stumble on the beach
littered with fronds and driftwood
and coconut husks,
and you follow the stalked eyes
of the tiptoeing ghost crabs
as if they were haunted—
that, too, is me.

When the hardest rains come
and you lift your head to the window
from a laptop or a book
in a shadowed corner,
to watch the rain trickle down
the drooping palm fronds
outside there in that western,
windblown storm,
and it suddenly feels like someone else
is there, dripping, with frog-green eyes
dissolving in green, green,
all the shades of green—
looking back in longing from
your windswept lanai, your rain-wet palm,
into your own wide eyes—yes.
That is me, it's me.

VI

A FEW SEASONS

SLO Creek Medicine

I wake, again, from a dream of war, swim awake,
sleepwalk out of the house into the City,
passing these other bodies like something blinded,
seeking the creek, like a steelhead turning home—
this other lost artery amid the traffic.
It tunnels under the streets like old medicine.
I sit on the creekbank, become a set of eyes . . .

and slowly the afternoon goes still
       and limpid,
pools and resettles, rounds itself
       languidly
deep in my brain. I could sit this way
       forever,
easing the dream away, easing it
       downslope
with the running creek . . .

Thick with the smell of anger,
the old silt settles . . . fists turn into shadows,
twisting like cottonwood leaves . . . bodies are
       pebbles . . .
smoke is the color of clusters of
       elderberries . . .
blood turns to water—
       the dream runs away, downhill . . .

I could sit forever,
       feeling the water slide
between my fingers,
       being this set of eyes.

I could sit forever
    watching the leaf-shapes change
    across the stones,
the swallowtail butterflies fall
    into the sky,
the black phoebe hunt upstream,
    downstream, upstream,
pressing to his white breast
    the white light on the stones
that, like himself, keeps moving
    all afternoon.

KINGFISHER

Blue and white flash
so deep in the City's heart
it's ridiculous:
the creeks channelized
years ago, concrete now,
stonewalled, officially
storm-drained;
and dry as my eyes are
in this five-year drought,
echoing, only full
of dead leaves, weeds,
dropped garbage,
abandoned grocery carts,
wheels up in despair—

that blue flash cutting across,
true as a dart
homing, skimming
the shrunken channel for
stains, wet tears
of seepage, one or two
forgotten places
under the looming culverts,
for flashes of fingerlings,
for oh, god! struck
to my senses, remembering
hope, seeing that
flash of ultramarine
so sure there's
a deep pool somewhere
hiding rainbows!

Growing Monarchs

Not having seen the god in any form
for months now, his resurrection
in question,
amid the trappings of this place
treading a ritual line, remembering
the things that must be remembered—
this is my task, it seems:
to water a dry garden, keep watering
long past midsummer, past the expected day,
the gray-green, tapered leaves
of the wild milkweed
I planted for him a year ago;
tore from the trackside,
put down white-weeping roots:
plant what he eats,
I figured—eventually
he'll come to feed.

Still, I watered half-heartedly until today,
when I saw the spray
curving around that fat, familiar form,
that thick lemon-and-black-striped caterpillar
immune to the beaks of birds,
hanging his promise from those bitter leaves,
that sleeping-case of pale jade rimmed with gold—
and at long, hard summer last,
the fire of his wings!

DRY AUGUST

Aaah! I am sick of the desert.
I need the green, the rain,
the vernal pools on the stretches
of flattened meadows,
I need the thick, rich mosses
muffling footsteps, the startling hue
of the fallen-sky-blue of lupines,
of baby-blue-eyes blossoms,
of wild grape hyacinths
in lakes under leafed-out oaks.

I need to see cavorting colts and calves
on grass-napped hillsides,
mule deer tiptoeing through
pearled veils of rain,
aaah, *rain*, whispering, dripping,
drumming its music
on logs and leaves, on dust-thick paths,
on boot-leather, hat-brims, bare palms
uplifted in gratitude, and upturned faces
with eyelids shut, but still
vulnerable to receive it, worship it,
thank it, to drink it in

like this thirsty dust I walk in,
this cracked-clay earth
that snakes to a flat horizon
that my dried-out, itching eyes
scan ceaselessly for clouds,
for flickers of lightning,
the smoke of far-off storms,

the flash-flood, the sky ablaze
with bone-white electrons—even
the monsoon, the deluge, the hurricane,
I don't care! I need *rain,*
rain! I need rain . . .

Flash Flood

Over the windowsill
across this empty table
through the coalescing air
comes the River

I drink this loud silence
I drink this poison
I drink this world splintering
I drink this remembering

Wasp in the distance
train two hours gone
dog singing in its sleep
the River comes

Knock at the heart-bones
gnat in the wrist's ear
stumble at the tongue-root
comes the River

Watch yourself leaving
locks fleeing doorframes
mud-heavy footsteps
one breath shaping another

Actinic sunlight
hard lines converging
narrows, condenses:
Fire. Stone. Water.

Like anything else
long sleeves empty
hanging out to dry
the River changes

Tap-dances, knuckles
laughs like an idiot
over its shoulder:
the River. Leaving.

THE OMENS OF AUTUMN

Early August. We've picked the first apples
from a tree bearing three crops—in January,
March and May. All three flowered
and set in separate stages. Bees were light
and few, whining among the petals
like drained ghosts, and dying on the paving-stones
before they carried the nectar home to feed
their hungry young, to build the waxy combs,
to swell them with pollen packed on hairy thighs—
hard workers, loaded for distance . . .

I found them, one by dying one, as if gravity
had stunned them, subtler than their own venom.
The first Canadian geese flew overhead
in late June, bellies fat as cargo planes,
their leveled wings guiding them down, earthward,
crying that ancient Egyptian wail, *Ankh! Ankh!*
from soul to heavily-laden soul, the chill
of northland downdrafts spilling
from high-summer-sky.

This night, the Perseids fling their lightning-bugs
against the dark, through veils of ocean-fog.
A deep tide swallowed the beaches, two days gone.
A red-cheeked band of small pelagic cormorants
harried the tidal bay, driving the fishes
into the shallows, to feed voraciously.
Two hundred miles south, we last saw them
treading the waters off the Channel Islands.

I pare the first large apple, ripe and green-skinned
and hard, the white flesh snapping from my teeth
that sample it. I will make apple sauce,
lattice-top pies and tarts, and crisps, and küchens,
and apple muffins, fragrant with cinnamon.
I'll freeze up half, crowding the smoking freezer
as if Spring wouldn't return—as if we'd need
reminders of how the honeybees used to drowse
among the blossoms, dozens and dozens of them—
as if we feared we would never hear again
the hum of the hiving, honey-making air . . .

At the nearby beach, the dead krill wash ashore
to litter the sand with bits of clotted blood.
Algae and other plankton disappear,
lost to the memories of starving whales.
I cannot imagine
an ocean finally flattened by oil and plastic . . .
Yet it's happening already: honeybees dying,
the apple tree bearing three crops,
the northern geese migrating
months before autumn,
the red tide blooming.

Under the Perseid showers, from far Gemini—
the mischief Twins—
I, having noticed Nature since childhood
on a farm, I have also noticed this:
these signs of revolving change; the mutterings
in the lees of staggering seasons,
drunk from the sun-storms and the borealis, both
grown hard against them. I can feel other planets
turn other faces to us, stars going nomad,
the galaxy's spiral loosening, the comets

crying long-distance signals, *ankh* to *ankh*,
soul to soul—these harbingers
of Time bleeding away . . .

My ageing body trembles. I sink my teeth
into these winter apples, as if that spark
a dying sun burns into them, burns my heart.
Head down, I concentrate on watching long
green peels under my paring-knife, echoing
the spirals of galaxies, the arms of harvest.
I'm weeping in August stillness, silently.
I'm weeping for all things caught in Time, measured
by days, by hours, by atoms—
for the long and terrible loss . . .
Tomorrow I must rise
to pick more winter apples,
hoping, like all mad creatures,
for the best.

AUTUMN

in the blank spaces
      between things
after the things themselves
are good and over
      seasons
long days into sunset
the walk together
August
and the shimmering wheat
this particular, this very
      afternoon
the taste of love
the black raspberry
the last light coppering
the ailanthus
      in between
the ending smell on the wind
the slice of moon
the cold sky going metal
against stars
      in between
the eyes
the open nostrils
the wind's fingers feeling
for the door
in the blood
      open, open
that stillness
at the throat's core
that sure coming
      inevitable, inevitable
that silence blooming
that cricket singing
in the veins

REAPER

Come gather me like a cornstalk
bend me sharply between nodes
rip my body from its rootlets
tear the seeds out of my throat

Come scythe me like a wheat-stem
break the reed of golden glass
crush the glume and awn and nutlet
for the uselessness it was

Axe my limbs like any orchard's
turn my leaves and fruits to stone
leave me bare to face the hoarfrost
when the dark of winter comes

But my seeds they are a thousand
grow a billion in my place
they lie hidden in your footsteps
spring like any blade of grass

mark your coming and your leaving
with a trodden trail of green
paint the pattern of your mayhem
each blade telling where you've been

Rest your head on any pillow
you will smother in your dreams
turn these fields to wrack and fallow
you will starve within the ruins

Come behead me with your talons
I will rise in winter rain
you will gnash your empty sockets
wish your black teeth back again

HOW SAD THE WIND SMELLS

How sad the wind smells today.
No matter the calendars crying summer,
it's the first day of autumn.
I can see the glint of green
going out
in your eyes,
and your birchbark-paper eyelids
droop and close,
as sunflowers turn from the star
that they were named for
to stare blindly at the ground.
So much, so beautiful
in the last daylight:
abandoned orb-weaver webs like power-lines
glinting, there-but-not-there, across
the impossibly-distant dust-brown hills,
diminishing into
the first of the winter rains.

PREMONITION 2: IN THE HILLS TONIGHT

Off in the hills tonight, dim thunder rumbling;
a late freight's cyclops eye groping down-grade;
the high, thin cries of wild geese chevroning.
Cumulus rising, suspending heavy water,
thrusting their shoulders upward into darkness,
metallic flashing of red-golden rimming
their high, pale mushroom heads. All else is dimness,
invisible. The hills crouch, blackened boulders,
all fires quenched, all daylight things illusions;
all beds unmade, all bouts canceled till dawn.
Lightning flares, retreats behind our eyelids.
What might be coming, the thickly-charged air tells us,
gliding across our skins, cooling, goose-fleshing.
We linger at open windows, breathe darkness in.
Cold hailstones touch our bodies, one by one.

COMES THE DARK

—for Bobbie

Comes late autumn,
light rivering from the sky,
dropping down-zodiac
with the headlong fall of time
passing, inevitable
as the beat of unseen wings.

Comes the dark,
blank as the stopped breath
lifted to a night sky
in the grip of winter,
holed with the glittering pain
of uncounted stars.

Comes December,
the frosted fur, the breath-ferns
on the windowpanes,
waking long before light to hold,
shivering,
the small flame of the heart
between numb hands.

Comes it all down to
the unwanted understanding
of the long fall of the Universe,
the dark at the galaxy's heart,
the flaming suns
singing their swan-songs, singing
against time, against gravity,
the far fire of their burning
tuned to our finite breaths.

VII

TURNING FOR HOME

On a Bicycle Again, after Twenty Years

The hills were broader than my mind,
the road ran farther than my fear.
I slowed to listen to the wind
and feel the breathing of the year

inside the hollows of my knees,
along the ridges of my bones.
Between the hurtling honeybees
and the hard glitter of the stones,

I spun a trail as thin as pain,
sobered, that it should come to pass
I'd hunger so to hear again
the sounds of August in the grass.

PRICE CANYON ROAD

A chilly early dawn in gray sea-fog,
we ride the canyon road to Pismo Beach.
You pedal beside me, dark beard hung with silver
droplets, bare leg hairs shining alike. The air
quivers around us, scented by oil-shale
seepage: we breathe in the dreams of dinosaurs;
the maple-syrup scent of everlasting
blooms, white puffs on etched stalks; anise smell
of fennel in the road's macadam cracks,
crushed by our slender wheel-rims. A white grin
opens your bearded face: you love this. Me,
I've not got your experience, your years
of riding: meets, half-centuries, competitions.

But I ride for this: the early morning chill
upon my heated face, this scented landscape
opening its lungs as I am opening mine.
Never mind numbers: mileage, speeds, gears,
to trot out and compare. Who really cares
about these things? I look for black-tailed deer
in foggy meadows; watch for hungry hawks
circling the low hills; eye deep-skirted oaks
rimming the fields, arms spread, blue chicory
and wild asters covering their feet.

You gesture at the rolling, curving road
ahead of us; you ask, "Okay with this?"
—knowing my limitations. "I'm okay,"
I breathe back, hard. "It's only wind and hills,
that's what kills me, wind and hills."
There's a wind around us now, but I already
know, you've reassured me: it's the wind
of our passing through here,
the wind of our passage only.

Remembering the Farm and Fern Hill

—apologies and all honor to Dylan Thomas

Oh sometimes it comes
sudden, uncalled for,
springing from the walled room
back of my eyes,
like a barn swallow rising: the Farm,
the Farm—and oh I am gone,
swallow-winged, crossing
wide fields with the shadows
of my flung hands touching, the pebbles
rolling under my tongue, sweet flame
of grasses, the wildwood, the owl,
the foxes, the dark hills, home as the nest
stuck under the eaves,
mouthed mud, tongued spittle of home;
and the shed wings lining the nest,
heart's down, stone-rooted, warm
all night long from the drunk-in sun,
and me in between—

Oh the Drunken One
already sang this
on another hill: the blunt-nosed,
heavy-blooded Dylan,
long gone dust—
that is not *my* name, no,
this is my name:
swallow, swallow,
swallow! and the singing
climbs in my throat,
a rain-swollen creek, heavy from
the source, a wind all through me

not named my name, a willing
tremor along my tongue-veins flowing,
rising, this holy singing
not of my own knowing only,
this going-on of an ancient thing
another laid down,
a stone on a hillside
for me to find,
blind, willy-nilly,
against all my senses, consenting.

Big Sur

Dropping down from Sierra pines
to the redwoods of the Coast,
the road curls like a gopher snake.
A red-tailed hawk climbs first

through a blown breath of ocean fog
then into enameled sun,
over cypress trees and the Bixby Bridge,
and the buckwheat's rusty bloom ...

And somewhere here the familiar feel
of my life comes back to me,
as the smell of dying kelp comes up
off a September sea.

ABOUT THE AUTHOR

Photo by B. J. Gingg

MARGUERITE COSTIGAN is a professional artist, naturalist, and life-long poet. She began writing poetry as a child on her artist-father's farm in rural Pennsylvania. In high school, her work was included in a national poetry anthology. A 44-year transplant to California, her poems embrace multiple themes: the human condition, the environment, war and love. Her work has appeared in *Blood and Thunder, Café Solo, Asylum*, the anthology *Poems for Endangered Places*, and the international journal *Le Fenetre*. She has taught with the California State Poets in the Schools program, has been reading her work live before Central Coast audiences since the 1970s, and was proclaimed San Luis Obispo County Poet Laureate 2015 and 2016 by the Board of Supervisors. Two of Marguerite's poetry collections have been published: *Rock & Fire* and *War & Whispers*. Marguerite lives in San Luis Obispo with her musician/writer husband and two plump cats.

www.ingramcontent.com/pod-product-compliance
Lightning Source LLC
Chambersburg PA
CBHW071353090426
42738CB00012B/3107